Contents

What is energy?

Energy makes things happen. It is how things move and change. Energy sends a car down the road. It turns on a lamp. Energy powers people too. The food we eat gives us the energy to work and play.

There are two types of energy. One is called potential energy. This energy is stored. The other is called kinetic energy. This energy moves.

The Sun's energy makes light and heat. Plants and animals need this to live and grow.

Smithsonian

LITTLE EXPLORER

Energy

by Melissa Higgins

Raintree is an imprint of Capstone Global Library Limited, a company incorporated in
England and Wales having its registered office at 264 Banbury Road, Oxford, OX2 7DY –
Registered company number: 6695582

www.raintree.co.uk
myorders@raintree.co.uk

Edited by Michelle Parkin
Designed by Kyle Grenz
Original illustrations © Capstone Global Library Limited 2020
Picture research by Eric Gohl
Production by Tori Abraham
Originated by Capstone Global Library Ltd
Printed and bound in India

978 1 4747 8705 5 (hardback)
978 1 4747 8710 9 (paperback)

British Library Cataloguing in Publication Data
A full catalogue record for this book is available from the British Library.

Acknowledgements
We would like to thank the following for permission to reproduce photographs: Alamy:
Phil Degginger, 22–23; NASA: 13 (inset); Shutterstock: AndreyUG, 20, Andris Barbans,
8, Blue Planet Studio, 19, brgfx, 25, Daniel Sockwell, 22 (inset), Dmitri Malyshev, 29
(left), Evannovostro, background (throughout), fotohunter, 4, Gansstock, 26–27, Janos
Rautonen, 26 (bottom), Jason Kolenda, 7, konmesa, 24, Love Silhouette, 16, Marian
Weyo, 11 (inset), Mark Agnor, 21, Mehaniq, 15, Mirko Graul, 29 (right), MonoLiza, 1,
muratart, 17, noraismail, 12–13, Ralf Beier, cover, Volodymyr Goinyk, 11, yotily, 12 (inset),
zhangyang, 5; Wikimedia: Public Domain, 6

Our very special thanks to Henry D. Winter III, PhD, Astrophysicist, Center for
Astrophysics, Harvard and Smithsonian. We would also like to thank Kealy Gordon,
Product Development Manager, and the following at Smithsonian Enterprises: Ellen
Nanney, Licensing Manager; Brigid Ferraro, Vice President, Education and Consumer
Products; and Carol LeBlanc, Senior Vice President, Education and Consumer Products.

Potential energy

A rock sits high on a cliff. It is not moving. The rock has potential energy. There are different types of potential energy, including chemical energy, gravity, nuclear energy and elastic energy.

An archer wants to shoot an arrow. He pulls back the bow's string. This string stores energy. The energy releases when the archer lets go.

Aristotle was the first person to write about potential energy, around 2,000 years ago. He was a philosopher who lived in ancient Greece.

Chemical energy

When you go camping, you use a match and wooden logs to start a fire. The logs burn because of chemical energy. Dry wood stores chemicals. When the wood is lit, these chemicals react with each other. The chemical reaction causes fire.

Chemical energy makes fire. It also makes a car go. Tiny sparks cause chemicals in petrol to explode. The small blasts power a car's engine.

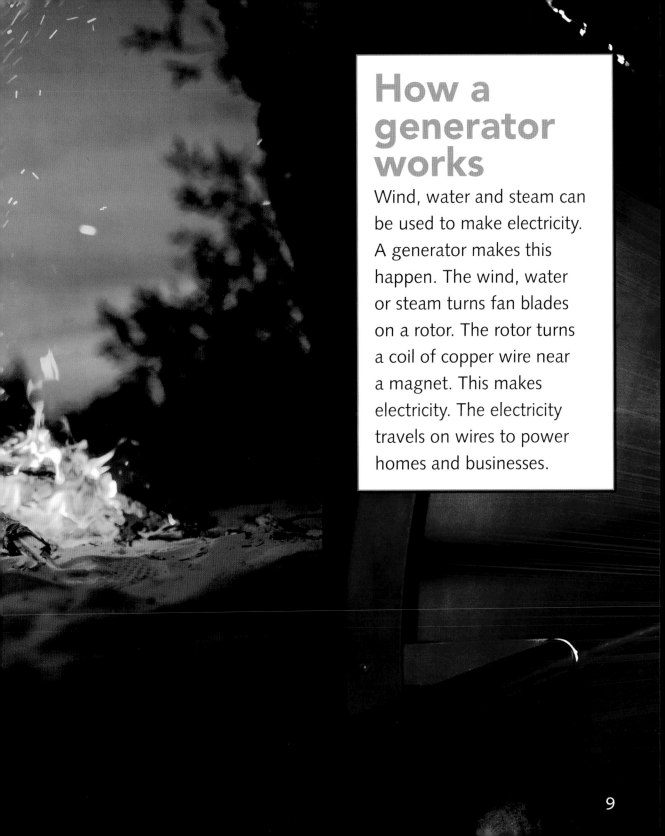

How a generator works

Wind, water and steam can be used to make electricity. A generator makes this happen. The wind, water or steam turns fan blades on a rotor. The rotor turns a coil of copper wire near a magnet. This makes electricity. The electricity travels on wires to power homes and businesses.

Gravity

Throw a ball up into the air. No matter how hard you throw it, the ball does not fly forever. At some point, the ball will fall to the ground. This is because of gravity. Gravity pulls objects together. Both the ball and Earth are objects. Earth pulls the ball towards its centre. Gravity works on people too. Because of Earth's gravity, we stay on the ground. We don't float away into space.

Larger objects such as planets have stronger gravitational pulls.

An apple on the ground does not have much potential energy. It has nowhere to fall. An apple on a tree branch has more potential energy. Because of gravity, the apple can fall from the tree to the ground.

Nuclear energy

Nuclear potential energy is also called atomic energy. This is because the energy is stored in the centre of atoms.

More than 30 countries around the world use nuclear energy.

Nuclear energy is very powerful. It moves submarines. It's used to make atomic bombs. Most of the nuclear energy that humans use is changed into electricity. A nuclear reactor splits atoms. This makes heat. The heat is used to make steam. A generator turns the moving steam into electricity.

The Curiosity rover on Mars is powered by nuclear energy.

Elastic energy

Stretch a rubber band. It has a strong tug. This is elastic energy. As you pull or twist, the rubber band stores energy. Springs store elastic energy when stretched or squeezed.

When let go, objects with elastic energy go back to their original shape. But there are limits. Bands and springs can wear out.

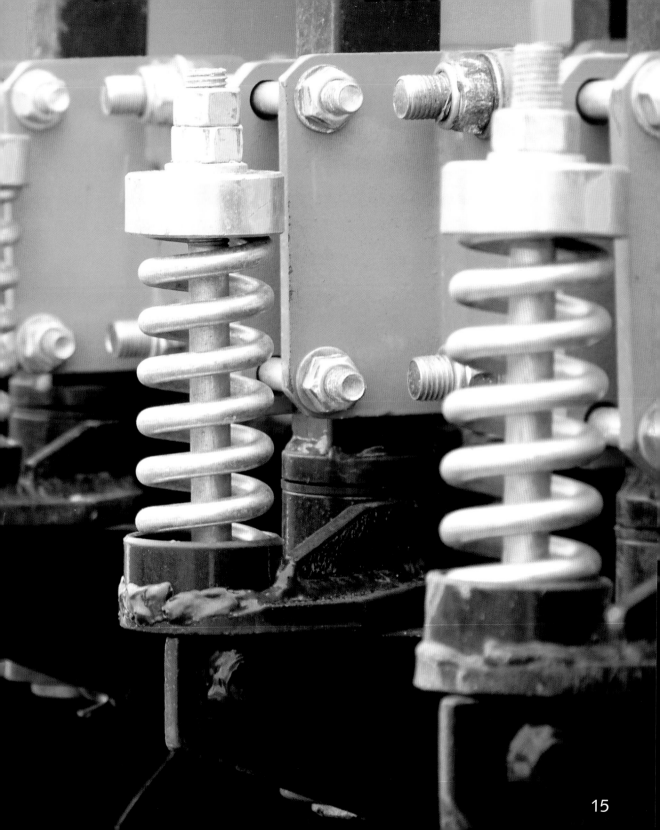

Kinetic energy

Do you remember the rock on the cliff? It's not moving. But what happens when a mountain goat kicks the rock off the edge? The falling rock's energy is no longer stored. It is moving. Moving energy is called kinetic energy.

There are five types of kinetic energy – mechanical, thermal, electrical, radiant and sound. Kinetic energy can be passed from one object to another. When you kick a football, your foot passes its energy to the ball.

The faster an object moves, the more kinetic energy it has. A bicycle rolling downhill gains kinetic energy.

Mechanical energy

An arrow flies. Car wheels turn. These objects have mechanical energy. That is the energy of moving things.

You can't see the wind. But it has mechanical energy. Wind turbines turn energy into electricity. Moving water has mechanical energy too. When water is turned into electricity, it is called hydroelectric power.

One large wind turbine makes enough electricity to power 1,400 homes. A big turbine can power 8,300 homes.

Renewable energy

The sun rises every day. Wind and water are always moving. These are sources of renewable energy. They do not run out. Coal, oil and gas are different. They take millions of years to form in the ground. Once used, they cannot be replaced. Many people are relying more and more on renewable energy.

Thermal energy

A saucepan of soup is on a hob. The soup warms because of thermal energy. This is the energy of moving atoms. When heated, atoms in the soup move faster. The faster they move, the hotter they get. When the hob is turned off, the atoms slow down. The soup cools.

Thermal energy is one of the oldest sources of power used by humans. Early humans lit fires to cook food and stay warm.

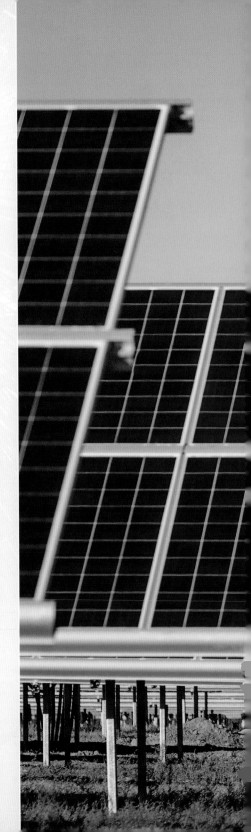

Solar thermal energy

The Sun's light can be used to make electricity and heat. Most solar panels collect sunlight and convert it to electricity. Solar thermal panels absorb the light to create thermal energy. A solar thermal farm can have hundreds of these panels. The panels absorb enough heat to make steam. Generators turn the steam into electricity for the farm.

Electrical energy

Many things in our world need electricity. Without it, ice cream would melt. Our food would not stay cool in the fridge. Lights would not turn on. Electrical energy is the movement of electrons. These particles flow along a path, like a wire. This path is called a circuit. The faster electrons move, the more energy they have.

Lightning is a form of electrical energy. Clouds fill with electrical charges. When the charges get big enough, they spark and make lightning.

A battery starts with potential energy. This turns into kinetic energy when the battery is connected to the circuit. Electrons move from one end of the battery to the other. This makes electricity.

Radiant energy

Radiant energy comes in many forms. X-rays are one form. Light is another. Radio waves are in this group too. Radiant energy is also called electromagnetic energy. This energy moves in waves. Electric waves travel up and down. Magnetic waves travel from side to side. Together they make radiant energy. Some waves are long. Others are short. Most cannot be seen.

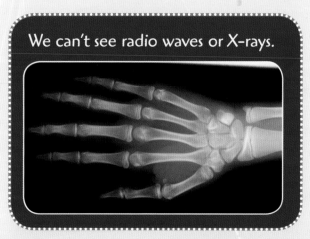

We can't see radio waves or X-rays.

Energy waves

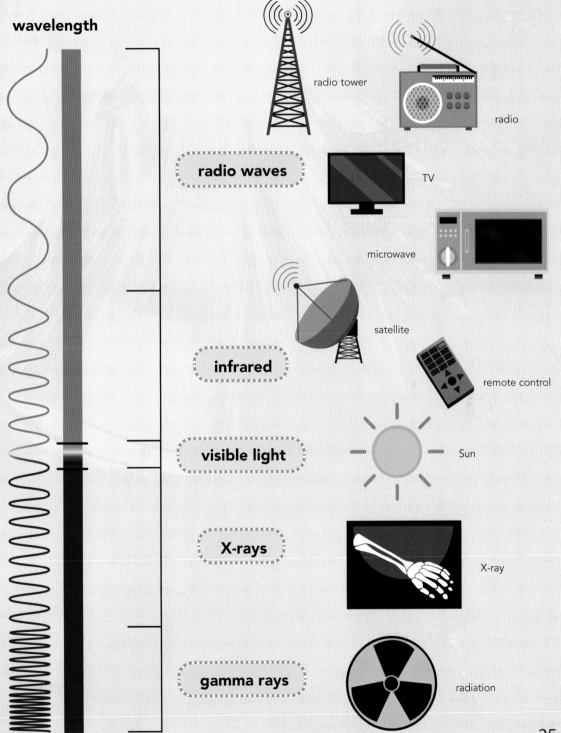

wavelength

radio tower

radio

radio waves

TV

microwave

satellite

infrared

remote control

visible light

Sun

X-rays

X-ray

gamma rays

radiation

Sound energy

We can hear sound. We can also feel it. Guitar strings vibrate when you strum them. Vibrating objects move back and forth very fast. Air particles nearby pick up the vibration.

Animals such as whales and dolphins use sound waves to find food and navigate in the dark ocean. This is called echolocation.

sperm whales

Like light, sound travels in waves. Sound waves move through many things, including air, water and many solid objects. These sound waves reach our ears. Nerves in our ears send signals to our brains. Then our brains identify the wave as a certain sound.

Sound waves travel slower than light waves. This is why you see a flash of lightning before you hear thunder.

Changing energy

Energy never ends. It changes from one form into another. The leaves of a potato plant take in radiant energy from the Sun. The potato stores it as chemical energy. A farmer uses mechanical energy to pick the plant. A man buys the potato from the farmer. The man's cooker heats up with electrical energy. It boils the potato using thermal energy. A girl eats the cooked potato for dinner. She goes outside and plays. Her body turns the food into mechanical energy.

The energy of the world is constant.

–Rudolf Clausius, physicist

Glossary

atom smallest form of an element

electron smallest particle within an atom

energy ability to do work, such as moving things or giving heat or light

generator machine that turns energy into electricity

hydroelectric making electric power from the force of moving water

particle tiny piece of something

philosopher person who studies truth and knowledge

rotor blade that spins around

sound wave wave that can be heard

submarine ship that can travel underwater

turbine machine with blades that can be turned by wind, steam or water

vibrate move back and forth quickly

Comprehension questions

1. There are two main types of energy. What are they?

2. A runner is set to start a race. What type of energy does she have?

3. Name two things that have elastic energy. What happens to those things when the energy is released?

Find out more

Books

All About Energy (All About Physics), Ella Newell (Raintree, 2020)

Energy (DK Eyewitness), Dan Green (DK Children, 2016)

From Crashing Waves to Music Download: An energy journey through the world of sound (Energy Journeys), Andrew Solway (Raintree, 2015)

Solar Energy (Energy Revolution), Karen Latchana Kenney (Raintree, 2020)

Websites

www.bbc.co.uk/bitesize/topics/zp22pv4/articles/ztxwqty
Learn more about renewable and non-renewable energy.

www.dkfindout.com/uk/video/human-body/how-much-energy-is-in-your-food-video
Watch this video to find out more about the energy in the food you eat.

Index